DeltaScienceReaders™

Food Chains and Webs

CONTENTS

What Is a Pond Ecosystem?

A pond may seem like a quiet place. But if you look carefully, you will see a lot of activity. Many different living things, or **organisms,** use the pond or make it their home. The pond is their **habitat.**

You will see many kinds, or **species,** of plants and animals. Deer drink at the water's edge. Cattails and grasses grow along the shore. Raccoons search for food, and turtles sun themselves. Lily pads and beetles float on the water. Schools of fish swim in the water.

A pond has many populations of organisms. A **population** is all the members of one species that live in the same area. All the cattails in a pond form a population of cattails. All the frogs in a pond form a population of frogs. Together, all the populations make up the pond **community.**

A pond has water and sand or mud at the bottom. A pond gets heat and light energy from the sun. These are nonliving things. Acting with each other, all the nonliving and living things form a pond **ecosystem.**

A pond is just one kind of ecosystem. Other kinds are forest, desert, saltwater, and grassland ecosystems.

Living Things Interact

The organisms in ecosystems **interact** in many ways. A fox interacts with a rabbit when it chases and catches it. A vine interacts with a tree when it grows and winds around it.

To stay alive, all animals need food. Some animals eat other animals. Foxes eat rabbits. The fox is a predator. A **predator** is an animal that kills and eats another animal. The rabbit is the fox's prey. The **prey** is the animal that is eaten. A frog is also a predator. Its prey may be an insect or a spider.

Some animals have special body parts or behaviors. These help them survive in their environments. A rabbit has long ears so it can hear danger and long legs so it can run fast. These **adaptations** help it survive. Owls have big eyes that let in a lot of light. This helps them see in the dark and find food at night.

A sea otter uses a rock to open an abalone. The abalone is its prey.

What adaptations can help a frog catch an insect? What adaptations might protect the insect?

Camouflage is an adaptation that helps keep some animals safe from predators. An animal with camouflage blends in with its environment. The animal's skin might have a pattern. The pattern may look like bark, leaves, or rock. The spots on a fawn's brown back are a kind of camouflage. They look like spots of sunlight among leaves and branches. They help the fawn hide in the forest.

Mimicry is another adaptation that helps some prey animals. Their shape and colored markings make them look much like another organism or object. One kind of fly looks like a wasp. This tricks birds. The birds do not eat the fly because they think it is a wasp. They don't want to be stung!

Organisms interact in other ways. A **parasite** lives in or on another living thing, called a **host.** A tick is a parasite. A tick lives on a dog or other animal and feeds on the host's blood.

The vine wrapped around the plant takes food from the plant.

The skin color of some lizards can change. What do you notice about the skin color of this lizard?

This kingsnake is not poisonous, but it looks like a poisonous coral snake.

5

Energy in an Ecosystem

Some birds fly thousands of miles every spring and fall. Imagine how much energy these birds need! They might get their energy from eating small insects. The insects get their energy by eating green plants. All living things need energy to live.

The sun is the source of energy for most life on Earth. Green plants are **producers.** They take in energy from the sun. They use this energy to make their own food. Grasses, oak trees, and tomato plants are producers. The food producers make contains **nutrients.**

All living things need nutrients in order to stay alive.

Animals cannot make their own food. They get energy by eating plants or other animals. Animals are **consumers.** Some consumers eat only plants. Some eat only animals. Other consumers eat both.

Decomposers are living things that get their energy from plants and animals that have died. Earthworms and mushrooms are decomposers. They break down the matter in dead organisms into smaller and smaller bits. Many of the nutrients return to the soil.

An **herbivore** eats only plants.

A **carnivore** eats other animals.

A **scavenger** eats dead organisms.

A **decomposer** breaks down dead organisms.

An **omnivore** eats both plants and animals. For example, birds eat insects and seeds.

Food Chains

A **food chain** shows how living things get food and energy. The energy source for almost all food chains is the sun. The first organism in a food chain is a producer. In a meadow, grass is a producer. Mice eat the grass, snakes eat the mice, and hawks eat the snakes.

When plants and animals die, they are broken down by decomposers. The nutrients returned to the soil can be used by the producers.

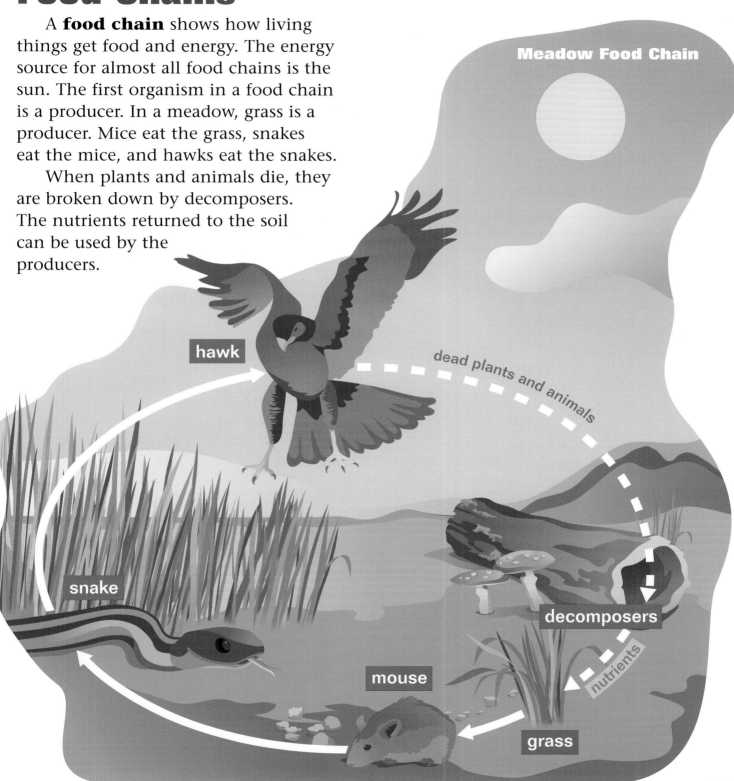

Meadow Food Chain

hawk

dead plants and animals

snake

decomposers

mouse

nutrients

grass

Food Webs

Often ecosystems have many food chains. Grass and mice live in a meadow, but so do birds, insects, and many other organisms. All the food chains in an ecosystem connect to form a **food web.**

A food web shows connecting food chains. What kinds of consumers do you see? What kind of producer do you see?

Meadow Food Web

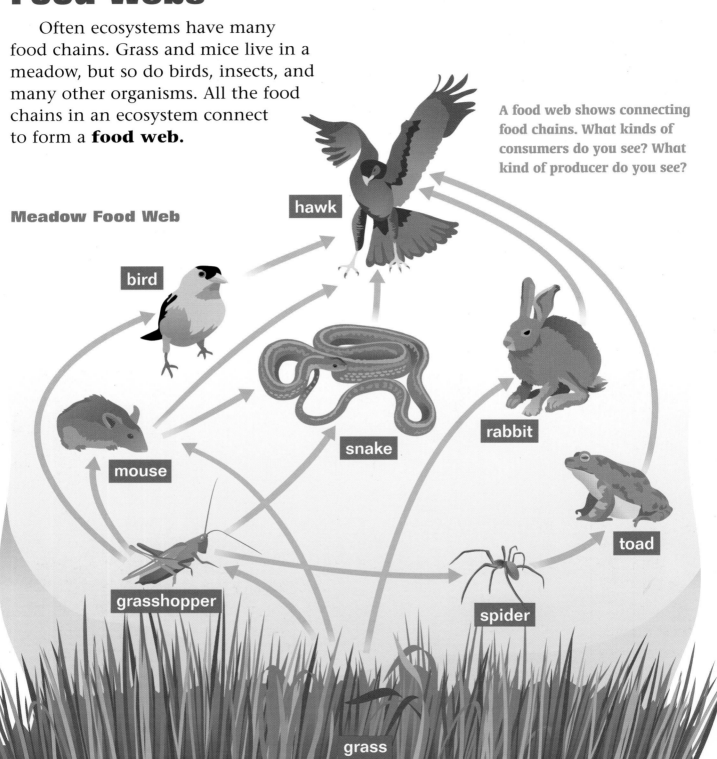

hawk

bird

mouse

snake

rabbit

grasshopper

spider

toad

grass

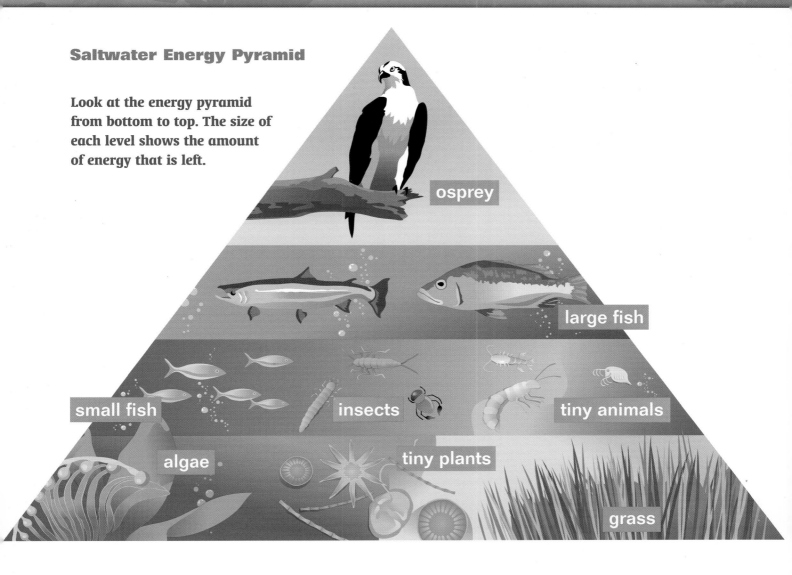

Saltwater Energy Pyramid

Look at the energy pyramid from bottom to top. The size of each level shows the amount of energy that is left.

osprey

large fish

small fish

insects

tiny animals

algae

tiny plants

grass

Energy Pyramids

A small fish eats algae. Algae are tiny plants that grow on coral and rocks. The fish gets energy from the nutrients in the algae. The fish uses the energy to move and grow. If an eel eats the fish, the eel will not get all the energy that first came from the algae. The fish has used up some of that energy.

An **energy pyramid** shows the amount of energy that moves through a food web. The producers are at the bottom of the pyramid. This level has the most energy. It also has the most organisms. Going up the pyramid, some energy is used up at each level. At the top of the pyramid, not much energy is left. Only a few animals are at the top. Energy flows through all ecosystems in much the same way.

Passenger pigeons were once common birds. Now they are extinct.

The grizzly bear is a threatened species.

A rain forest ecosystem has great diversity. It has many species of plants and animals.

How Do Ecosystems Change?

Sometimes places change. Change may happen slowly. A pond may fill in with dirt and dead leaves. After many years, the pond is gone and the area has become a meadow. Change can also happen fast. Lightning strikes and starts a forest fire. In just a few days, trees and wildlife are gone.

Plant and animal populations change, too. Sometimes many members of a species die or are killed. The species may become threatened, like the grizzly bear. Or the species may become **endangered,** like the blue whale. Very few are left. If all the members of a species die, the species becomes **extinct.** Dinosaurs became extinct long ago.

Diversity is the number of species in an area. A field of corn usually has only a few species. A meadow has hundreds. A rain forest has thousands. Diversity makes an ecosystem strong. Small changes are less likely to affect the whole ecosystem. If a disease attacks one corn plant, the disease could easily spread. It could kill most of the other corn plants in the field. If a disease attacks one kind of tree in a rain forest, that species might be the only kind to die. The disease might not harm the other trees that are different species.

Charles Darwin (1809–1882)

In 1831 the HMS *Beagle* left England. The ship was headed for South America to map the coast. Charles Darwin was on board. He was only 22 years old. The ship was to take him away from home for two years. But Darwin was excited. He had always loved nature. Now he would be studying the organisms in every place the ship stopped.

At every port Darwin went into the country. He studied thousands of plants and animals. He took samples. He drew pictures and wrote notes. No one had ever studied many of these organisms before. Most people had never even heard of them.

The *Beagle* stopped at the Galápagos Islands in the Pacific Ocean. Darwin was amazed at the diversity of life. Among the birds, he found thirteen species of finches. Each species had a different beak. Each ate a different food. Darwin learned that these adaptations allowed all these birds to live in one area.

The *Beagle's* trip lasted five years instead of two. The ship sailed all the way around the world. The voyage helped people realize that there is great diversity of life on Earth.

The HMS BEAGLE sailed to the Galápagos Islands.

Rachel Carson (1907–1964)

Rachel Carson was an author and scientist. She started writing when she was a child. Her first story was printed when she was in fourth grade, and she never stopped writing. In college she studied plants and animals. She also loved the sea and wrote three books about marine life.

Rachel Carson knew that living things interact. At that time, certain poisons were used to kill unwanted insects. She worried about these poisons. She thought some bird species were threatened because of them. In 1962 Rachel Carson warned people about the poisons in her book *Silent Spring*. In this book the word *ecosystem* was used for the first time. Her book helped people learn about how living things interact. The book helped people think about the environment.

Ecologists

This ecologist is at work measuring wind speed high above the treetops.

Ecologists study the living world and the environment. They learn how living things interact. They find out how nonliving things affect plants and animals. Some ecologists work in labs. Others work outdoors.

Some ecologists study forests. Above the treetops, they measure nonliving things like the amount of light and the wind speed. They place special buckets around the forest to catch leaves or insects. Back in the lab, they study the samples from the forest. Ecologists used this method in a rain forest. Their collection kept them busy for years. They found many insect species that had never been studied before.

Ecologists have to be good at observing. They need to keep track of what they see. They keep journals. They often write about their work. Some teach others about their research.

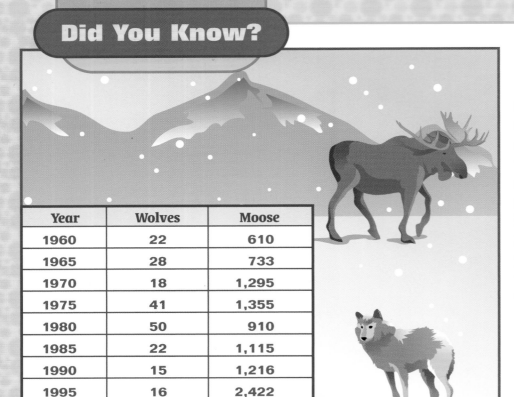

Year	Wolves	Moose
1960	22	610
1965	28	733
1970	18	1,295
1975	41	1,355
1980	50	910
1985	22	1,115
1990	15	1,216
1995	16	2,422
2000	29	850

Scientists count the wolves and moose on Isle Royale from airplanes. They count in the winter, when the trees are bare and tracks can be seen in the snow. Some of the wolves wear radio collars that give their location. When was the wolf population the smallest? When was the moose population the largest?

About Wolves and Moose on Isle Royale

Wolves and moose are two species on an island in Lake Superior. For over 40 years ecologists counted the number of moose and wolves on Isle Royale. The wolves are predators. The moose are their prey. Ecologists learned that the size of one population affects the size of the other.

When the moose population was high, the wolves had plenty to eat. So the number of wolves went up.

With more wolves, more moose were killed for food. This caused the number of moose to go down. It soon became harder for wolves to find prey. Then the number of wolves went down. With fewer predators, the number of moose began to go up. The cycle started again.

Other things also can affect population size. A long, cold winter can kill a lot of moose. Disease can kill both moose and wolves.

About Mountain Ecosystems

You can go from one ecosystem to another. One way is to hike up a mountain! Imagine you are at the base of an Arizona mountain. The air is warm and dry. Cactuses and shrubs are part of a desert scrub ecosystem.

As you make your way up the mountain, the air will grow cooler. The amount of rain that falls will increase. These changes affect the kinds of plants that live on the mountain.

Next you will pass through a grassland ecosystem. Short, dry grasses cover the ground. Then you will notice more and more trees. You will enter an oak woodland ecosystem and then a mixed pine and oak ecosystem. Farther up the mountain, you will find cool mixed conifer, or evergreen, forests. You will walk beneath large pine and fir trees, as well as some oaks. As you near the summit, the forest will begin to thin out and the trees will be shorter. You will climb through a spruce and fir ecosystem.

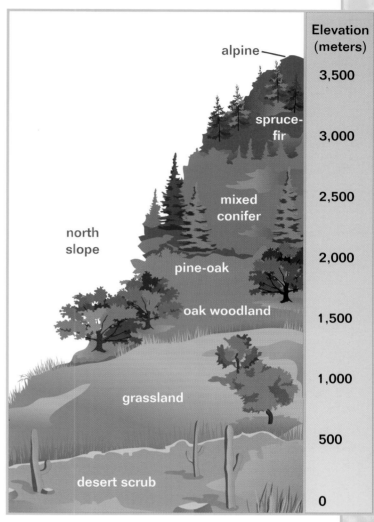

How many ecosystems does this mountain have?

When you climb to the top of the mountain, you will be above the timberline. With no trees to block the view, you can see for miles. It is cold and windy here. In this alpine ecosystem, only small flowers, shrubs, mosses, and some grasses can live.

Glossary

adaptation special body feature or behavior that helps an organism stay alive

camouflage adaptation that helps an organism blend in with its surroundings

carnivore consumer that eats only animals

community all the populations living in one area

consumer organism that eats other organisms in a food chain

decomposer organism that feeds on and breaks down dead organisms

diversity the number of different species in an area

ecosystem all the interacting living and nonliving things in one area

endangered in danger of becoming extinct

energy pyramid shows how energy moves through a food web

environment everything around a living thing

extinct species that has disappeared from Earth

food chain shows how organisms get food and energy

food web all the food chains in an ecosystem

habitat the area in which an organism lives

herbivore consumer that eats only plants

host organism that a parasite lives in or on

interact to act with each other

mimicry adaptation in which an organism looks like another organism or thing

nutrients things in food that organisms need to live

omnivore consumer that eats either plants or animals

organism living thing

parasite organism that lives in or on another organism and gets its food from it

population all the members of a species living in one area

predator animal that kills and eats other animals

prey animal that is killed and eaten by other animals

producer organism that makes its own food and serves as a source of food for other organisms

scavenger consumer that eats dead plants or animals

species group of organisms that are the same